THANKSGIVING
IN THE
WOODS

By Phyllis Alsdurf

Illustrations by Jenny Løvlie

Every Thanksgiving for more than twenty years, a family
in upstate New York has hosted an outdoor Thanksgiving feast
in the woods on their farm. Almost 200 friends, relatives, and
newcomers join in the festivities each year, regardless of the
weather. They bring food to share in a rustic, woodland setting with
bonfires for keeping warm and tarps overhead as protection from the
snow or rain. It's a time of great celebration and joy, with music and
singing filling the air for this Thanksgiving in the Woods.

When fall winds blow cold
and jack-o-lanterns lose their smiles,
when branches lie bare,
and corn stalks rustle in the wind,

that's when it's time for
Thanksgiving in the Woods.

Days and days go by, and I keep
adding to my Thanksgiving pile—

a tool belt and my favorite rocks,
a rope, seashells, a flashlight,
and Brownie—

everything I'll need for
Thanksgiving in the Woods.

One chilly morning Mama wakes me early.
"Today's the day," she says.

I stuff all of my treasures into a backpack.
Mama gathers boots and winter coats.

Daddy grabs his guitar and my recorder. "Come on," he says. "Let's get going to Thanksgiving in the Woods!"

We drive and drive and finally
turn onto a curvy gravel road.
That's when I see Grandpa
standing next to his orange truck.

He starts the engine,
and I climb into the cab.
Time to get ready for
Thanksgiving in the Woods!

We drive over rutted fields,
then down a slope to a clearing
under trees that reach
to the clouds.

I see the cousins
building a fort right
next to the little stream—
a perfect place for our own
Thanksgiving in the Woods.

Daddy and Grandpa unload
long wooden planks for tables
and bales of straw for us to sit on.

Uncle Charlie makes a bonfire
while neighbors hoist a tarp over branches.
Everyone's rushing to get ready for
Thanksgiving in the Woods.

Early the next morning
I'm one of the first ones to
wake up. I can hardly wait
for breakfast to be done.

While grown-ups laugh and talk,
kids pull on sweaters and boots.
We want to get there first for
Thanksgiving in the Woods.

Some neighbors are already at the site. "Here, help stack up some kindling," Grandpa says. And we do, running whenever someone calls.

We all need to help
if we're going to have
Thanksgiving in the Woods.

Soon a tractor comes over the hill.
Grandma and Mama sit on the hay wagon
steadying a load of pots and covered pans
filled with turkeys and dressing,
mashed potatoes, peas, and corn.

Oh, now it's starting to
smell like Thanksgiving
in the Woods!

Neighbors, relatives,
and lots of people I don't
even know cross the field
to the hollow under
the hemlocks.

They carry baskets and
bags and boxes filled with
apples and pickles and pies—
every imaginable food to share
for Thanksgiving in the Woods.

At one o'clock Grandma rings her special bell.
We form a huge circle and sing:
'Tis the gift to be simple, 'Tis the gift to be free.
People talk for a long time about being thankful.

Brownie gets very hungry waiting until it's time to start Thanksgiving in the Woods.

Lines of people snake around the tables,
filling plates with mounds of food.

The cousins and I dart in and out, grabbing buns, turkey, and other treats we take to our fort. There we'll have our own Thanksgiving in the Woods.

Grown-ups are playing fiddles,
banjos, and drums and singing songs
that everyone knows.

Soon Daddy joins in on his guitar, and I make up a tune of my own on my recorder—my way of celebrating Thanksgiving in the Woods.

We stand around the bonfire,
warming up on both sides.

Grandma passes out marshmallows,
and I take two to roast toasty and brown—
one of my favorite parts about
Thanksgiving in the Woods.

When everyone's had
enough turkey and potatoes
and pumpkin pie, people
start packing up their gear.

In groups of two or three they walk back to the farmyard, bringing an end to Thanksgiving in the Woods.

Daddy puts me on his shoulders,
and we walk with Mama
and Grandma along a candlelit
path through the woods.

I pull Brownie close to keep
him warm, happy that he came along
for Thanksgiving in the Woods.

Back at the bonfire
I can hear a banjo
and someone singing:
'Tis the gift to be simple,
'tis the gift to be free,
'Tis the gift to come down
where we ought to be.

"Now that's a perfect ending," Grandma says as we walk in the dusk, "a perfect ending to Thanksgiving in the Woods."

Simple Gifts

Joseph Brackett, 1848
a Shaker from Maine

Phyllis Alsdurf grew up on a Southern Minnesota dairy farm where one of her chores was to run down the lane and bring the cows up to the barn for milking. In addition to *Thanksgiving in the Woods*, she is the author of *It's Milking Time* (Random House, 2012). Phyllis is a former journalism and creative writing professor at Bethel University and lives in the Twin Cities with her husband, Jim, and miniature Golden Doodle, Lloyd.

Jenny Løvlie is a Norwegian illustrator, designer, creative, foodie, and bird enthusiast! Her work is fun and colorful with lots of animals, brave kids, and plants in all shapes and sizes. Jenny is fascinated by the strong bond between humans, animals and nature.

For Dick and Shari Gibbs and the Hidley House Thanksgiving crew.
—P.A.

First edition published 2017
    Printed in the USA

JUN2018

23 22 21 20 19 18   2 3 4 5 6 7 8

ISBN: 978-1-5064-2508-5

Library of Congress Cataloging-in-Publication Data

Names: Alsdurf, Phyllis, 1950- author. |Løvlie, Jenny, illustrator.
Title: Thanksgiving in the Woods / by Phyllis Alsdurf ; illustrated by Jenny
  Lovlie.
Description: First edition. | Minneapolis, MN : Sparkhouse Family, 2017. |
  Summary: A boy relates the preparations for, and enjoyment of, his
  family's annual Thanksgiving in the Woods celebration on his grandparents'
  farm. Includes words to the Shaker hymn, Tis a Gift to be Simple, and
  notes about the real gathering on which the story is based.
Identifiers: LCCN 2017007995 | ISBN 9781506425085 (hardcover : alk. paper)
Subjects: | CYAC: Family life--Fiction. | Thanksgiving Day--Fiction.
Classification: LCC PZ7.A46263 Th 2017 | DDC [E]--dc23
LC record available at https://lccn.loc.gov/2017007995

Sparkhouse Family
510 Marquette Avenue
Minneapolis, MN 55402
sparkhouse.org